W9-ATO-052

WITHDRAWN

12/05

# NEW YORK

Written by Ann Heinrichs    Illustrated by Matt Kania
Content Adviser: Jennifer Murphy, Head of the Children's Room,
Albany Public Library, Albany, New York

Published in the United States of America by The Child's World®
PO Box 326 • Chanhassen, MN 55317-0326
800-599-READ • www.childsworld.com

**Photo Credits**
Cover: Kathleen Petelinsek; frontispiece: Digital Vision.

Interior: Corbis: 9 (James L. Amos), 10 (Annie Griffiths Belt), 13 (Werner Forman), 17 (Larry Lee Photography), 18 (Bettmann), 30 (Gail Mooney); Erie Canal Village: 22; The Farmer's Museum: 21; Getty Images/The Image Bank/ Pete Turner: 26; National Baseball Hall of Fame, Cooperstown, New York: 34; Photodisc: 6, 29; Lee Snider/Photo Images/Corbis: 14, 33; Bob Wagoner/ Corning Museum of Glass: 25.

**Acknowledgments**
The Child's World®: Mary Berendes, Publishing Director

Editorial Directions, Inc.: E. Russell Primm, Editorial Director; Katie Marsico, Associate Editor; Judith Shiffer, Assistant Editor; Matt Messbarger, Editorial Assistant; Susan Hindman, Copy Editor; Melissa McDaniel, Proofreader; Kevin Cunningham, Peter Garnham, Matt Messbarger, Olivia Nellums, Chris Simms, Molly Symmonds, Katherine Trickle, Carl Stephen Wender, Fact Checkers; Tim Griffin/IndexServ, Indexer; Cian Loughlin O'Day, Photo Researcher and Editor

The Design Lab: Kathleen Petelinsek, Design and art production

Library of Congress Cataloging-in-Publication Data
Heinrichs, Ann.
   New York / by Ann Heinrichs.
      p. cm. — (Welcome to the U.S.A.)
   Includes index.
   ISBN 1-59296-380-3 (library bound : alk. paper) 1. New York (State)—Juvenile literature. I. Title.
   F119.3.H453 2006
   974.7'044—dc22                    2005000532

Ann Heinrichs is the author of more than 100 books for children and young adults. She has also enjoyed successful careers as a children's book editor and an advertising copywriter. Ann grew up in Fort Smith, Arkansas, and lives in Chicago, Illinois.

About the Author
Ann Heinrichs

Matt Kania loves maps and, as a kid, dreamed of making them. In school he studied geography and cartography, and today he makes maps for a living. Matt's favorite thing about drawing maps is learning about the places they represent. Many of the maps he has created can be found in books, magazines, videos, Web sites, and public places.

About the
Map Illustrator
Matt Kania

On the cover: **The Statue of Liberty is a sign of freedom to all who see her.**
On page one: **The Hudson River Valley is beautiful any time of the year.**

# OUR NEW YORK TRIP

4

WELCOME TO
NEW YORK

**R**eady for a tour of the Empire State? That's New York! Now, New York City is pretty famous. But just wait. New York State is really great!

Take this trip, and you'll ride a ship. You'll spin thread and blow glass. You'll stand beneath thundering waterfalls. You'll roam among foxes and deer. You'll climb sand dunes and see the Statue of Liberty. And you'll watch the Headless Horseman riding by!

Does that sound like a fun tour? Then buckle your seat belt. We're on our way!

As you travel through New York, watch for all the interesting facts along the way.

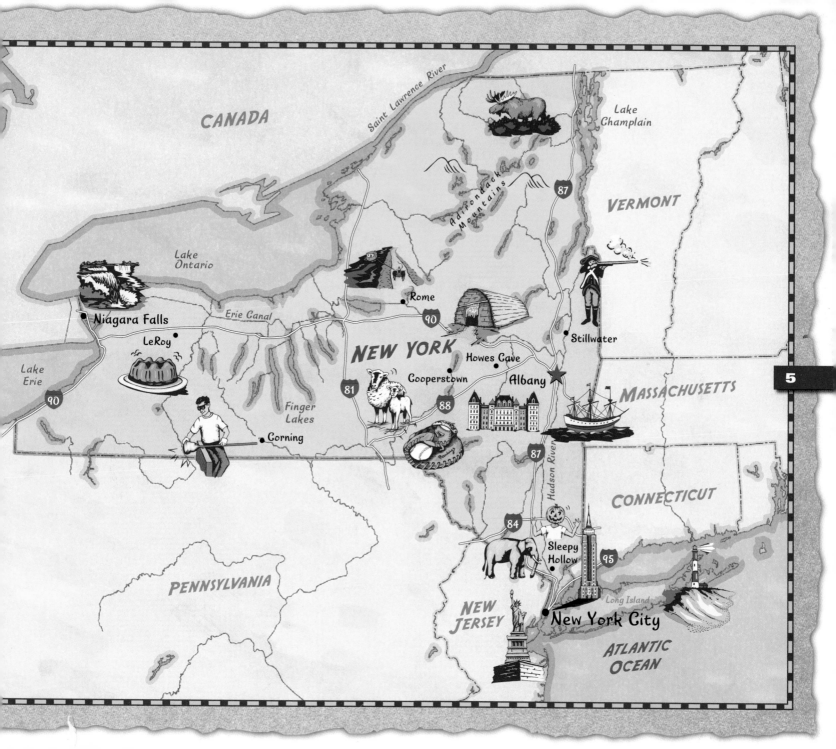

CANADA

Saint Lawrence River

Lake Champlain

Adirondack Mountains

VERMONT

87

Lake Ontario

Erie Canal

Rome

90

Niagara Falls

LeRoy

Stillwater

NEW YORK

Howes Cave

MASSACHUSETTS

Lake Erie

90

81

Cooperstown

Finger Lakes

88

Albany

Corning

87

Hudson River

CONNECTICUT

95

84

Sleepy Hollow

PENNSYLVANIA

NEW JERSEY

New York City

Long Island

ATLANTIC OCEAN

Want to see Niagara Falls up close? Just take a boat tour!

Niagara Falls lies partly in the United States and partly in Canada.

## Getting Close to Niagara Falls

**P**ut on your poncho. Then follow the guide. Soon you're right at the base of Niagara Falls. The water crashes in a thundering roar!

Niagara Falls is a waterfall on the Niagara River. This river connects Lake Erie and Lake Ontario. Lake Ontario flows into the Saint Lawrence River. This river eventually empties into the Atlantic Ocean. The Hudson River reaches the Atlantic, too. It flows down the state from north to south.

The Adirondack Mountains rise in the northeast. Farther south are the Catskill Mountains. Many lakes are scattered through the state. The Finger Lakes are long and thin—like fingers!

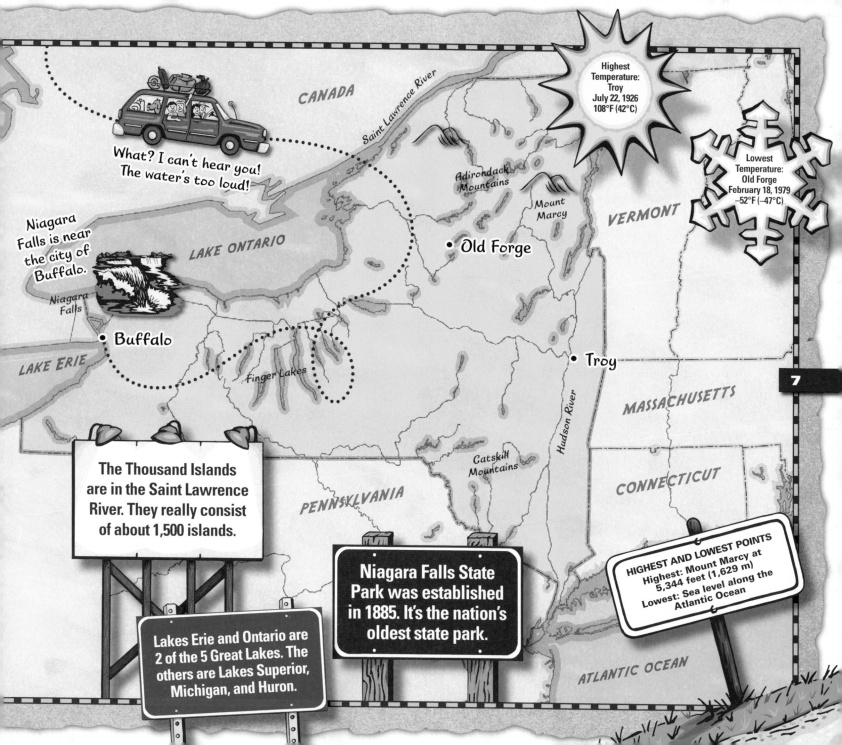

CANADA

Saint Lawrence River

Highest
Temperature:
Troy
July 22, 1926
108°F (42°C)

Lowest
Temperature:
Old Forge
February 18, 1979
-52°F (-47°C)

Adirondack
Mountains

Mount
Marcy

VERMONT

• Old Forge

What? I can't hear you!
The water's too loud!

Niagara
Falls is near
the city of
Buffalo.

LAKE ONTARIO

Niagara
Falls

• Buffalo

LAKE ERIE

Finger Lakes

• Troy

7

Hudson River

MASSACHUSETTS

Catskill
Mountains

CONNECTICUT

PENNSYLVANIA

The Thousand Islands
are in the Saint Lawrence
River. They really consist
of about 1,500 islands.

Niagara Falls State
Park was established
in 1885. It's the nation's
oldest state park.

HIGHEST AND LOWEST POINTS
Highest: Mount Marcy at
5,344 feet (1,629 m)
Lowest: Sea level along the
Atlantic Ocean

Lakes Erie and Ontario are
2 of the 5 Great Lakes. The
others are Lakes Superior,
Michigan, and Huron.

ATLANTIC OCEAN

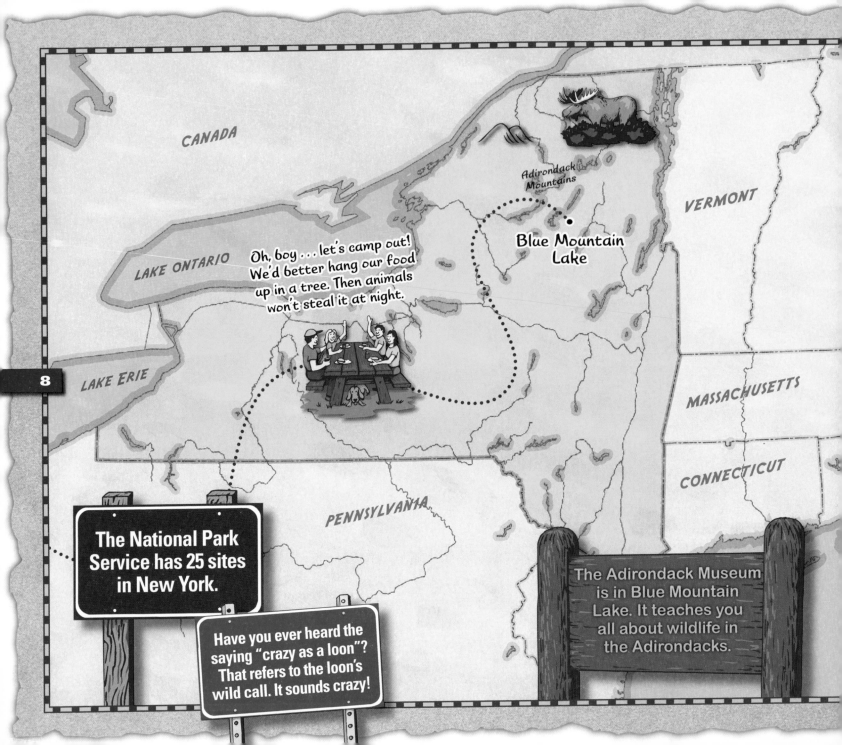

CANADA

VERMONT

Adirondack
Mountains

Blue Mountain
Lake

LAKE ONTARIO

Oh, boy ... let's camp out!
We'd better hang our food
up in a tree. Then animals
won't steal it at night.

MASSACHUSETTS

LAKE ERIE

8

CONNECTICUT

PENNSYLVANIA

**The National Park
Service has 25 sites
in New York.**

Have you ever heard the
saying "crazy as a loon"?
That refers to the loon's
wild call. It sounds crazy!

The Adirondack Museum
is in Blue Mountain
Lake. It teaches you
all about wildlife in
the Adirondacks.

## Wildlife Watching in the Adirondacks

**W**alk softly through the Adirondacks. You'll hear lots of animal sounds. Chipmunks and squirrels are chirping. Frogs and toads are croaking. A loud, cackling noise may startle you. It sounds like really crazy laughing. That's a waterbird called a loon.

Deer and moose live in the Adirondack forests. Lots of beavers live there, too. They build homes along the water. The homes look like big mounds of sticks.

Black bears and bobcats lurk in the forest. You may not see them, though. They're very shy!

This loon's home is in the Adirondacks.

STATE FLOWER
ROSE

STATE TREE
SUGAR MAPLE

STATE BIRD
BLUEBIRD

Now, let's see. It's long.
And it's an island. It must
be Long Island!

**C**limb the high sand dunes. Watch the ocean from a sandy beach. Roam through forests where deer and foxes live. You're on Fire Island. It's protected as a national seashore. It stretches alongside Long Island.

Long Island lies off New York's southeast coast. It has many communities. The island's western end is busy and crowded. The eastern end is much quieter. There you'll see farms and fishing villages.

Beaches stretch along much of the south shore. The north shore was once called the Gold Coast. Many rich people built summer homes there. Some of those homes are now museums.

Deer on the beach? This is not an uncommon sight on Fire Island.

10

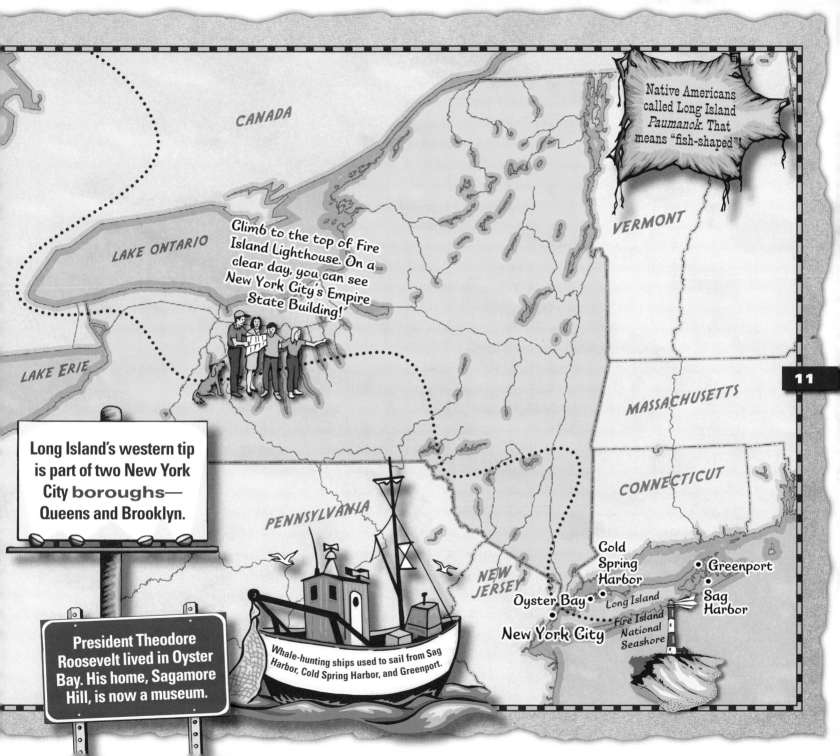

CANADA

LAKE ONTARIO

LAKE ERIE

VERMONT

MASSACHUSETTS

CONNECTICUT

PENNSYLVANIA

NEW JERSEY

Native Americans called Long Island *Paumanok*. That means "fish-shaped"!

Climb to the top of Fire Island Lighthouse. On a clear day, you can see New York City's Empire State Building!

Long Island's western tip is part of two New York City boroughs— Queens and Brooklyn.

President Theodore Roosevelt lived in Oyster Bay. His home, Sagamore Hill, is now a museum.

Whale-hunting ships used to sail from Sag Harbor, Cold Spring Harbor, and Greenport.

Cold Spring Harbor

Greenport

Oyster Bay

Long Island

Sag Harbor

New York City

Fire Island National Seashore

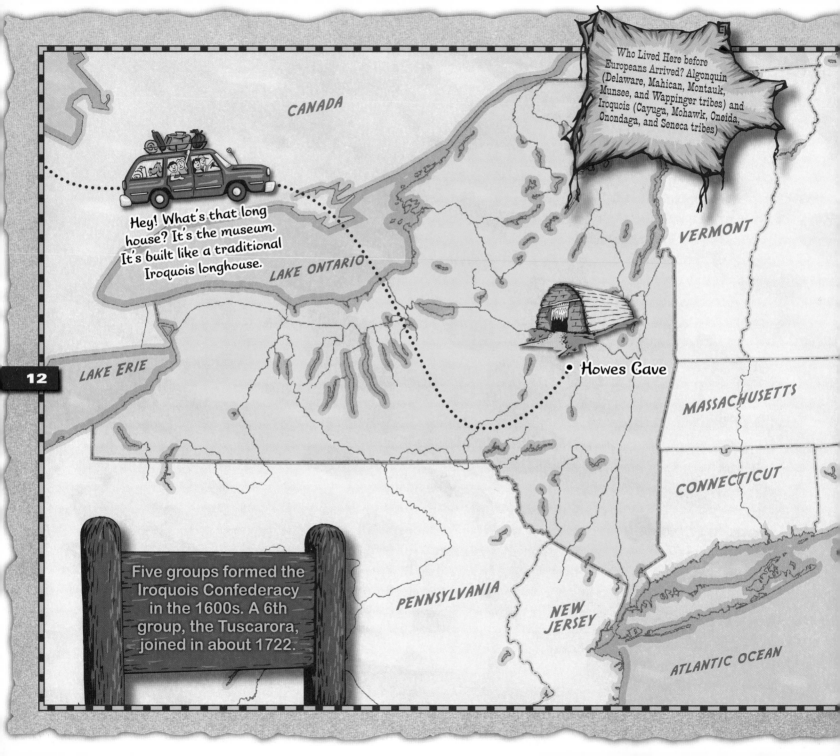

**M**ake a doll out of corn **husks.** Pound corn into cornmeal. Hear American Indian **legends** from long ago.

You're visiting the Iroquois Indian Museum. There you learn about the Iroquois way of life. You can even try out their **traditional** activities.

The Iroquois were made up of five groups. They lived in New York before Europeans arrived. Iroquois built longhouses as homes. They raised corn, beans, and squash. The Iroquois respected the natural world. They hunted only for food.

Algonquin people lived in New York, too. They also were a union of several groups.

Would you wear this mask on Halloween? The Iroquois made it long ago.

13

The Dutch bought Manhattan Island from the Indians. How much did they pay? Less than $25!

Would you have been a good explorer? Hop aboard the *Half Moon* and find out!

You can tour many old Dutch homes in New York. They include Wyckoff House, Philipsburg Manor, and the Bronck Museum.

## Half Moon Tours on the Hudson

**C**limb aboard the ship. High atop the mast is the crow's nest. That's where sailors perched to see far away. Soon you're sailing down the Hudson River!

You're taking a tour on the *Half Moon*. It's built like Henry Hudson's ship the *Half Moon*. Hudson sailed to present-day New York in 1609. He claimed it for the Netherlands. This new land was named New Netherland.

Many **Dutch** settlers soon moved in. They founded Fort Orange in 1624. It became Albany. They also founded New Amsterdam. It's now New York City.

The English took over the region in 1664. They named it New York. It became one of the thirteen English **colonies.**

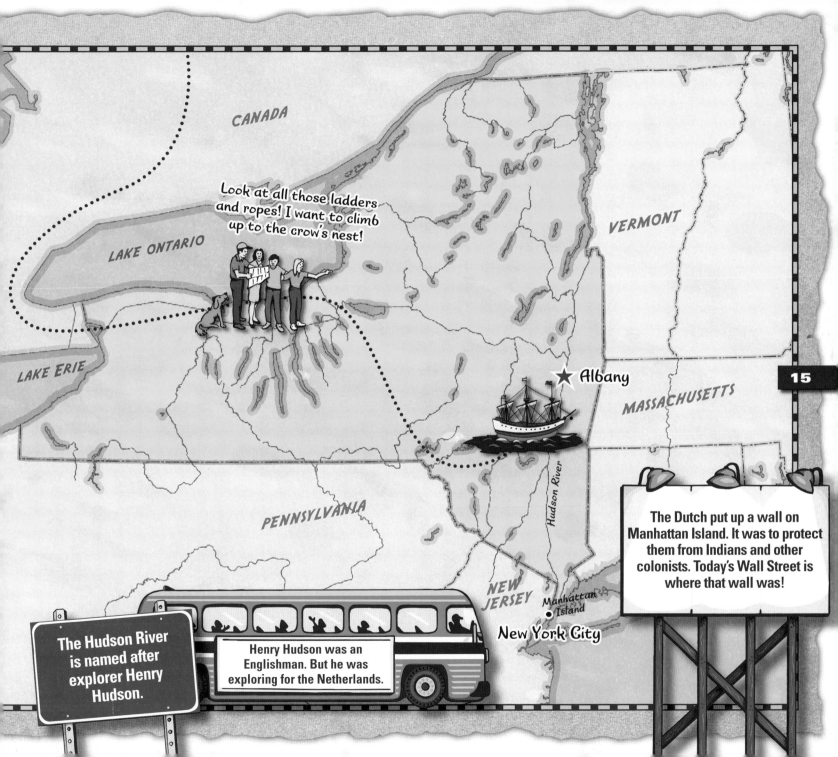

CANADA

LAKE ONTARIO

LAKE ERIE

VERMONT

★ Albany

MASSACHUSETTS

Look at all those ladders and ropes! I want to climb up to the crow's nest!

PENNSYLVANIA

Hudson River

NEW JERSEY

Manhattan Island

New York City

The Dutch put up a wall on Manhattan Island. It was to protect them from Indians and other colonists. Today's Wall Street is where that wall was!

The Hudson River is named after explorer Henry Hudson.

Henry Hudson was an Englishman. But he was exploring for the Netherlands.

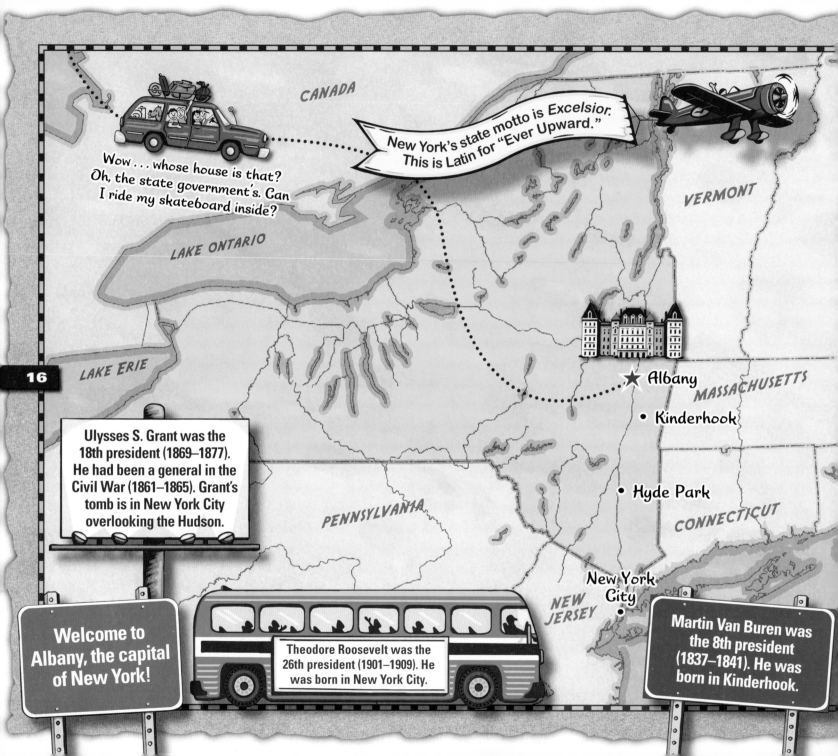

CANADA

New York's state motto is Excelsior. This is Latin for "Ever Upward."

Wow . . . whose house is that? Oh, the state government's. Can I ride my skateboard inside?

LAKE ONTARIO

VERMONT

16

LAKE ERIE

★ Albany

MASSACHUSETTS

• Kinderhook

Ulysses S. Grant was the 18th president (1869–1877). He had been a general in the Civil War (1861–1865). Grant's tomb is in New York City overlooking the Hudson.

• Hyde Park

PENNSYLVANIA

CONNECTICUT

New York City

NEW JERSEY

**Welcome to Albany, the capital of New York!**

Theodore Roosevelt was the 26th president (1901–1909). He was born in New York City.

**Martin Van Buren was the 8th president (1837–1841). He was born in Kinderhook.**

## The State Capitol in Albany

The state capitol is huge. It covers more ground than two football fields! Inside, it's like a beautiful castle. Its tall columns reach up to high ceilings. You'll see stained-glass windows and rich, dark wood. The state government offices are in this building.

All states have three branches of government. New York is no different. One branch makes the state laws. Another branch carries out those laws. It's headed by the governor. The third branch consists of judges. They listen to cases in court. Then they decide whether laws have been broken.

Is this a palace? No, it's the capitol in Albany!

17

Franklin D. Roosevelt was the 32nd president (1933–1945). He was born in Hyde Park.

The Battle of Saratoga took place in 1777.

New York was the 11th state to enter the Union. It joined on July 26, 1788.

## The Battle of Saratoga at Stillwater

**C**annons are booming. **Muskets** are firing. Want to be a British soldier? Or want to join the American side? How about being a spy?

You're at Saratoga Battlefield. People are acting out the Battle of Saratoga. Everyone is dressed in 1700s clothes. Even kids can take part in the action.

This battle took place during the Revolutionary War (1775–1783). Colonists were fighting for freedom from Great Britain. They won! The thirteen colonies became the first thirteen states.

General George Washington had the colonial army. He became the first U.S. president. And New York City became the nation's capital!

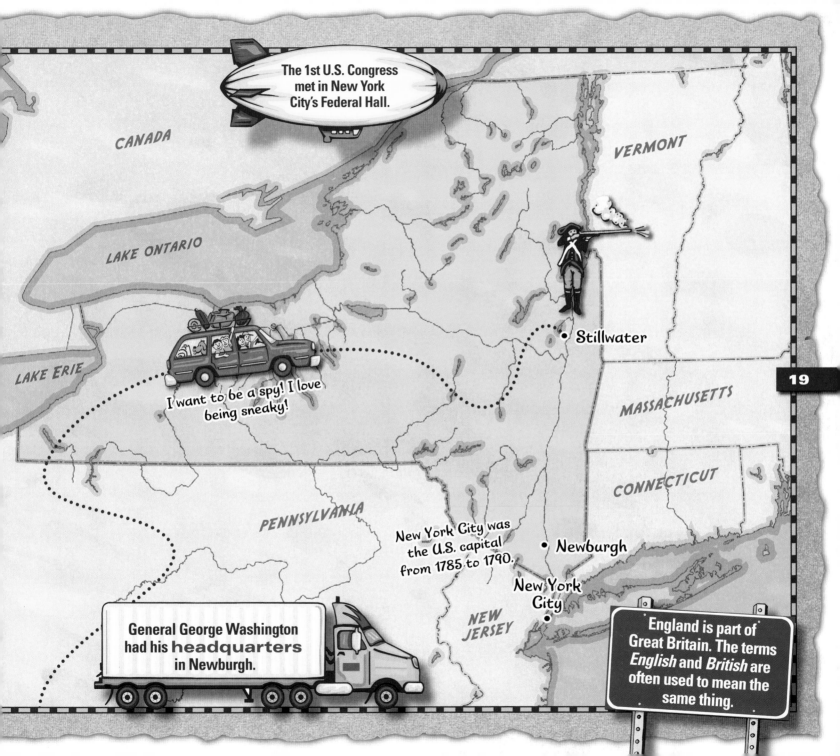

The 1st U.S. Congress met in New York City's Federal Hall.

CANADA

VERMONT

LAKE ONTARIO

LAKE ERIE

● Stillwater

I want to be a spy! I love being sneaky!

MASSACHUSETTS

CONNECTICUT

PENNSYLVANIA

New York City was the U.S. capital from 1785 to 1790.

● Newburgh

New York City

NEW JERSEY

General George Washington had his **headquarters** in Newburgh.

England is part of Great Britain. The terms *English* and *British* are often used to mean the same thing.

CANADA

Only California and Wisconsin produce more milk than New York.

Hey . . . let's pet those big, woolly sheep. See those red pigs? Look at those huge duck eggs!

LAKE ONTARIO

VERMONT

Syracuse •

The state fair is held in Syracuse from late August through early September each year.

• Cooperstown

LAKE ERIE

20

MASSACHUSETTS

CONNECTICUT

PENNSYLVANIA

Only California and Washington State produce more grapes than New York.

What Does New York Raise? Milk and dairy products, cattle, and chickens

What Are New York's Fishing Products? Oysters, clams, bluefish, striped bass, perch, trout, and salmon

# The Farmers' Museum in Cooperstown

**H**ere's someone making a broom. There's someone hammering hot metal into tools. Others are carving wood or making candles. You can join in, too. Try your hand at spinning **flax** into thread.

You're enjoying a day at Village Crossroads. It's part of the Farmers' Museum. It shows how New York farmers once lived.

New York farmers are still busy today. Many of them raise dairy cattle. Dairy cows are good at producing milk. Milk is New York's leading farm product.

Other farmers grow fruits and vegetables. Do you like apples? Your next apple might come from New York. It's a top apple-growing state.

Want to learn how to spin thread? Visit the Farmers' Museum in Cooperstown.

Only Washington State produces more apples than New York.

## Riding Down the Erie Canal in Rome

**Y**ou're riding a big, wooden boat. It seems like you're on a skinny river. But it's really a **canal.** Horses are walking along the bank. They are pulling the boat with a rope!

You're visiting Erie Canal Village. And you're riding down the Erie Canal. What a great way to travel!

New York farmers liked the canal, too. So did factory owners. There were few roads in the 1800s. It cost a lot to ship goods by land.

The Erie Canal opened in 1825. It joined Lake Erie to the Hudson River. Then it became much easier to ship goods. New York soon led the nation in trade.

22

Giddyap! Horses are pulling this boat along the canal.

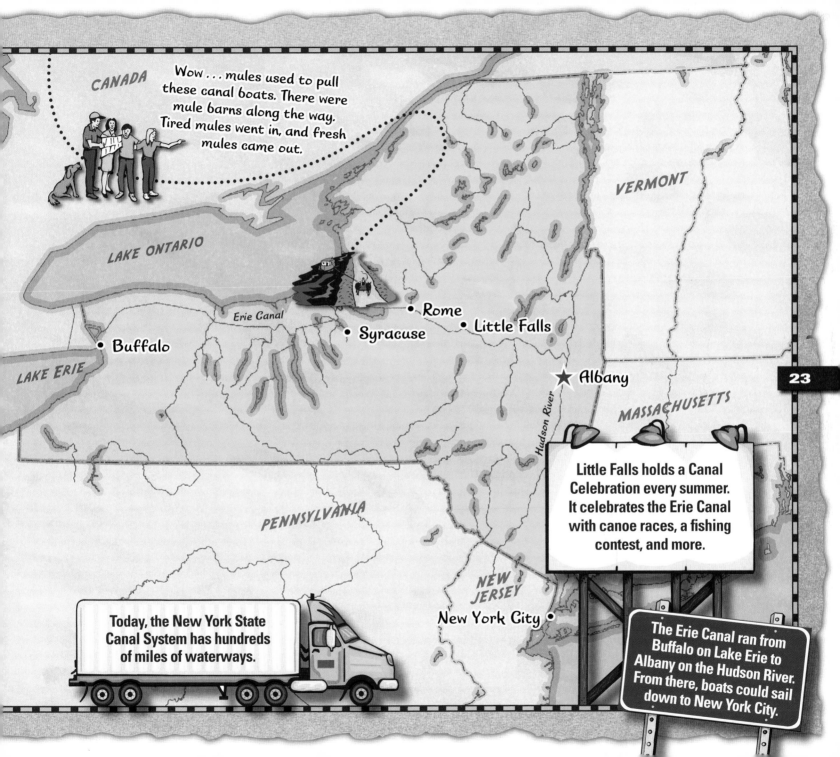

Wow... mules used to pull these canal boats. There were mule barns along the way. Tired mules went in, and fresh mules came out.

CANADA

LAKE ONTARIO

VERMONT

Erie Canal

• Rome

• Buffalo

• Syracuse

• Little Falls

LAKE ERIE

★ Albany

Hudson River

MASSACHUSETTS

Little Falls holds a Canal Celebration every summer. It celebrates the Erie Canal with canoe races, a fishing contest, and more.

PENNSYLVANIA

NEW JERSEY

New York City •

Today, the New York State Canal System has hundreds of miles of waterways.

The Erie Canal ran from Buffalo on Lake Erie to Albany on the Hudson River. From there, boats could sail down to New York City.

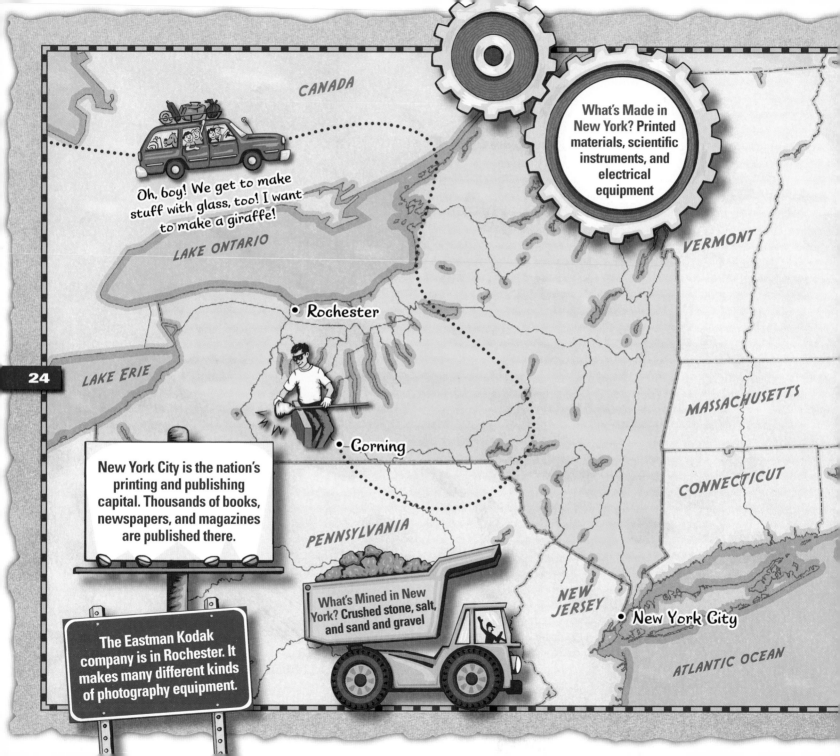

CANADA

Oh, boy! We get to make stuff with glass, too! I want to make a giraffe!

LAKE ONTARIO

What's Made in New York? Printed materials, scientific instruments, and electrical equipment

VERMONT

• Rochester

LAKE ERIE

24

MASSACHUSETTS

• Corning

New York City is the nation's printing and publishing capital. Thousands of books, newspapers, and magazines are published there.

CONNECTICUT

PENNSYLVANIA

The Eastman Kodak company is in Rochester. It makes many different kinds of photography equipment.

What's Mined in New York? Crushed stone, salt, and sand and gravel

NEW JERSEY

• New York City

ATLANTIC OCEAN

Blobbing is a way to decorate glass. You drop blobs of melted glass onto a glass surface.

Visitors enjoy the Hot Glass Show in Corning.

**W**atch the master glassblowers. They melt the glass till it's stretchy. They blow into a tube to add air. Then they pull and fold it into shapes. Presto! There's a glass fish!

You're watching the Hot Glass Show. It happens at the Corning Museum of Glass. Its glassblowers make glass the old-fashioned way.

New Yorkers once made lots of things by hand. Today, factories do most of the work. New York's factories make medicines and machines. Some make cameras, film, and copy machines. Others make parts for computers or cars. Food, clothes, and books are New York products, too.

25

The Statue of Liberty was a gift from France.

**Ellis Island was open for immigration from 1892 to 1954. About 12 million immigrants arrived during that time.**

## The Statue of Liberty in New York Harbor

There she stands in New York Harbor. She's the Statue of Liberty. Millions of **immigrants** saw her as they arrived. She's a sign of freedom in a new land.

Near the statue is Ellis Island. New immigrants used to register there. In the late 1800s, thousands of people arrived. Many settled right in New York. Some had come from Italy, Ireland, or Germany. Others were from Poland or Russia.

Today, New Yorkers have roots in many countries. They come from Europe, Asia, and Africa. Many come from Spanish-speaking lands. They all have special foods, music, and customs. New York life would be boring without them!

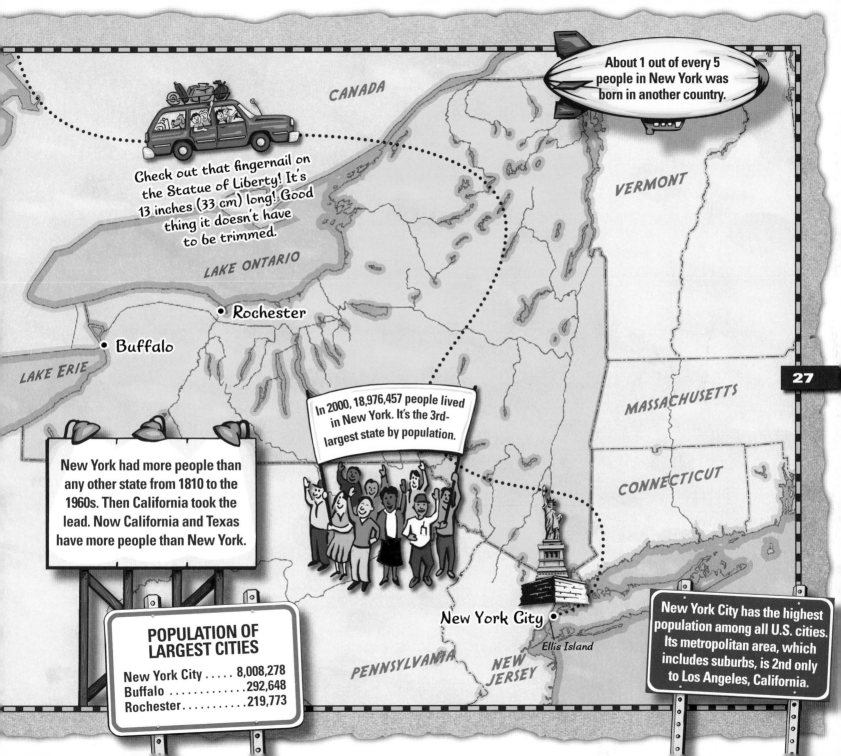

CANADA

About 1 out of every 5 people in New York was born in another country.

Check out that fingernail on the Statue of Liberty! It's 13 inches (33 cm) long! Good thing it doesn't have to be trimmed.

VERMONT

LAKE ONTARIO

• Rochester

• Buffalo

LAKE ERIE

MASSACHUSETTS

In 2000, 18,976,457 people lived in New York. It's the 3rd-largest state by population.

CONNECTICUT

New York had more people than any other state from 1810 to the 1960s. Then California took the lead. Now California and Texas have more people than New York.

New York City •

Ellis Island

PENNSYLVANIA

NEW JERSEY

New York City has the highest population among all U.S. cities. Its metropolitan area, which includes suburbs, is 2nd only to Los Angeles, California.

## POPULATION OF LARGEST CITIES

New York City . . . . . 8,008,278
Buffalo . . . . . . . . . . . . 292,648
Rochester . . . . . . . . . 219,773

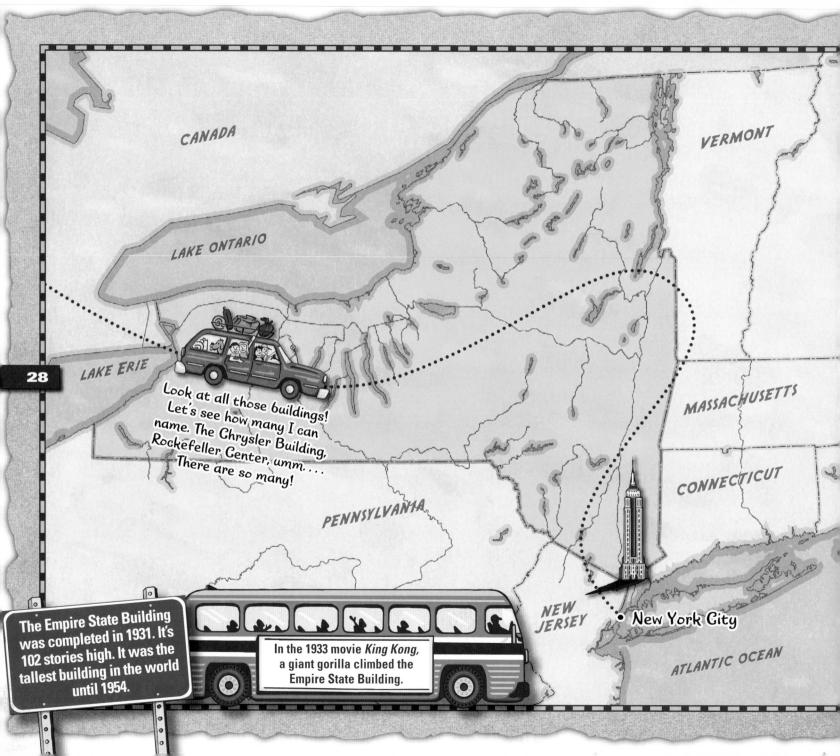

CANADA

VERMONT

LAKE ONTARIO

LAKE ERIE

MASSACHUSETTS

Look at all those buildings! Let's see how many I can name. The Chrysler Building, Rockefeller Center, umm. . . . There are so many!

CONNECTICUT

PENNSYLVANIA

NEW JERSEY

• New York City

The Empire State Building was completed in 1931. It's 102 stories high. It was the tallest building in the world until 1954.

In the 1933 movie *King Kong*, a giant gorilla climbed the Empire State Building.

ATLANTIC OCEAN

Visit the Empire State Building. Take the elevators to the top. Walk around the deck and gaze out. You see tall buildings everywhere. You may see rivers and mountains, too.

It's easy to imagine you're a king or queen. That helps you understand New York's nickname. It's called the Empire State. An empire is a huge kingdom.

New York grew to become a very important state. It's one of the top manufacturing states. It's also a leading center for music and art. Many TV networks and banks have their headquarters there.

New York became a world center, too. The United Nations was formed in 1945. It made New York City its home.

The Empire State Building opened in 1931. More than 3.5 million people visit it every year.

29

Study dinosaur fossils at the American Museum of Natural History.

**E**xplore the world of dinosaurs. Learn about ancient ways of healing. Find out how elephants live. You're at the American Museum of Natural History!

New York City has jillions of cool places. You'll see plays and musicals on Broadway. You'll shop for funky clothes in Greenwich Village. You can eat in Chinatown or Little Italy. Rockefeller Center is popular in the winter. People go ice skating in its outdoor rink.

All these places are on Manhattan Island. Manhattan is just one of the city's boroughs. The others are Brooklyn, the Bronx, Queens, and Staten Island.

La Guardia and John F. Kennedy are airports in Queens.

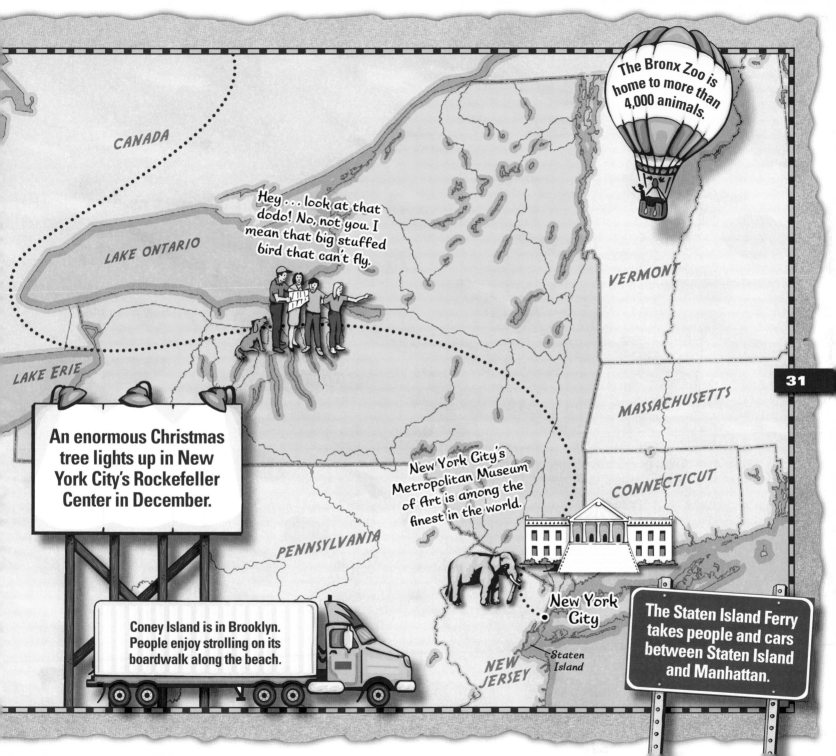

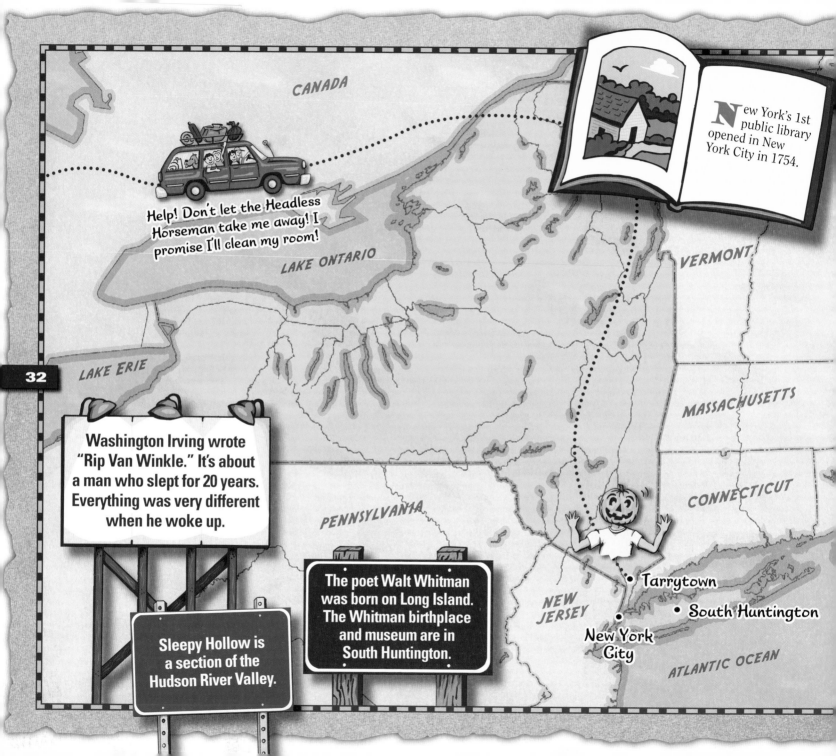

CANADA

LAKE ONTARIO

Help! Don't let the Headless Horseman take me away! I promise I'll clean my room!

New York's 1st public library opened in New York City in 1754.

VERMONT

LAKE ERIE

32

MASSACHUSETTS

Washington Irving wrote "Rip Van Winkle." It's about a man who slept for 20 years. Everything was very different when he woke up.

PENNSYLVANIA

CONNECTICUT

The poet Walt Whitman was born on Long Island. The Whitman birthplace and museum are in South Huntington.

Sleepy Hollow is a section of the Hudson River Valley.

Tarrytown

NEW JERSEY

South Huntington

New York City

ATLANTIC OCEAN

## Halloween in Sleepy Hollow

**G**hosts and witches are roaming around. A storyteller is telling scary stories. Look—the Headless Horseman is riding by!

Don't worry. It's Halloween time at Philipsburg Manor. This old home is near Tarrytown. It's in an area called Sleepy Hollow.

The Headless Horseman lives only in storybooks. He appears in "The Legend of Sleepy Hollow." That's a spooky tale by Washington Irving.

Irving himself lived in the Sleepy Hollow area. People can visit his home, called Sunnyside. Scary things happen there on Halloween, too!

Would you dare to visit Sunnyside on Halloween?

Dutch people settled in Sleepy Hollow in the 1600s. Some of Washington Irving's tales are based on old Dutch legends.

Are you good at baseball? Maybe someday you'll be in the Hall of Fame!

Joe Jackson played for the Chicago White Sox. Once, his new shoes hurt his feet. So he ran the bases without shoes. After that, his nickname became Shoeless Joe.

## Cooperstown's Baseball Hall of Fame

What does Sammy Sosa's bat look like? How about "Shoeless" Joe Jackson's glove?

You'll find out all this and more. Just stop by the Baseball Hall of Fame!

Baseball is one of New Yorkers' favorite sports. The Yankees and Mets are the home teams. Fans of both teams are very loyal. They fight about who's better!

Team sports are fun to watch. But New York has lots more to offer. Winter's the time for skiing and snowmobiling. Summer brings people to the beaches and lakes. Any time's great for hiking through the forests. New York has something for everyone!

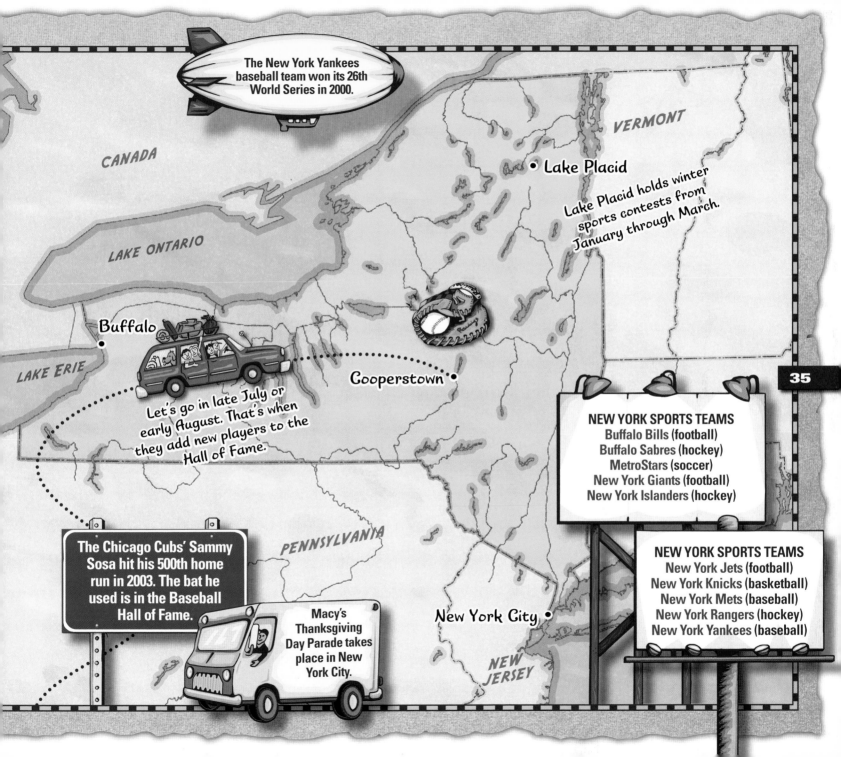

The New York Yankees baseball team won its 26th World Series in 2000.

CANADA

VERMONT

Lake Placid

Lake Placid holds winter sports contests from January through March.

LAKE ONTARIO

Buffalo

LAKE ERIE

Let's go in late July or early August. That's when they add new players to the Hall of Fame.

Cooperstown

**NEW YORK SPORTS TEAMS**
Buffalo Bills (football)
Buffalo Sabres (hockey)
MetroStars (soccer)
New York Giants (football)
New York Islanders (hockey)

PENNSYLVANIA

The Chicago Cubs' Sammy Sosa hit his 500th home run in 2003. The bat he used is in the Baseball Hall of Fame.

Macy's Thanksgiving Day Parade takes place in New York City.

New York City

NEW JERSEY

**NEW YORK SPORTS TEAMS**
New York Jets (football)
New York Knicks (basketball)
New York Mets (baseball)
New York Rangers (hockey)
New York Yankees (baseball)

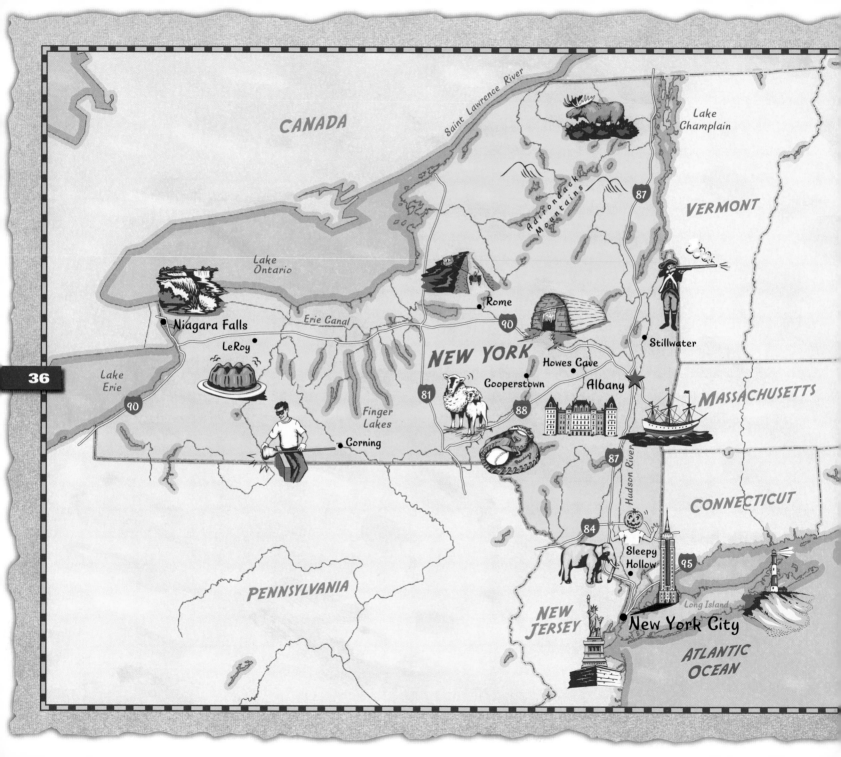

CANADA

Saint Lawrence River

Lake Champlain

VERMONT

Lake Ontario

Adirondack Mountains

87

Erie Canal

Rome

Niagara Falls

90

LeRoy

Stillwater

**NEW YORK**

Howes Cave

Lake Erie

90

81

Cooperstown

Albany

MASSACHUSETTS

Finger Lakes

88

Corning

CONNECTICUT

Hudson River

87

84

Sleepy Hollow

95

PENNSYLVANIA

Long Island

NEW JERSEY

New York City

ATLANTIC OCEAN

## OUR TRIP

We visited many amazing places on our trip! We also met a lot of interesting people along the way. Look at the map on the left. Use your finger to trace all the places we have been.

Where is Niagara Falls located? See page 7 for the answer.

Who called Long Island *Paumanok*? Page 11 has the answer.

How many Native American groups formed the Iroquois Confederacy? See page 12 for the answer.

How much money did the Dutch pay for Manhattan Island? Look on page 14 for the answer.

Which states produce more milk than New York? Page 20 has the answer.

How many people arrived at Ellis Island from 1892 to 1954? Turn to page 26 for the answer.

What is New York's largest city? Look on page 27 and find out!

What famous parade takes place in New York City? Turn to page 35 for the answer.

That was a great trip! We have traveled all over New York!

There are a few places that we didn't have time for, though. Next time, we plan to visit the Jell-O Museum in LeRoy. The museum provides information on the history of Jell-O. Exhibits include television ads featuring stars such as Bill Cosby and Lucille Ball.

More Places to Visit in New York

## WORDS TO KNOW

**boroughs** (BUR-ohz) towns or sections that make up a large city

**canal** (kuh-NAL) a long, narrow waterway dug by humans

**colonies** (KOL-uh-neez) lands with ties to a mother country

**Dutch** (DUCH) having to do with the Netherlands

**flax** (FLAKS) a plant with fibers that can be made into thread

**headquarters** (HED-kwor-turz) a group's main office or meeting place

**husks** (HUHSKS) rough outer coverings

**immigrants** (IM-uh-gruhnts) people who leave their home country and move to another land

**legends** (LEJ-uhndz) old tales told to teach a lesson or explain something

**muskets** (MUHSS-kits) heavy guns used in the Revolutionary War

**traditional** (truh-DISH-uhn-uhl) following long-held customs

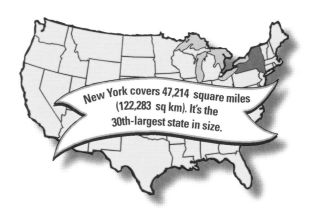

New York covers 47,214 square miles (122,283 sq km). It's the 30th-largest state in size.

## STATE SYMBOLS

**State animal:** Beaver

**State beverage:** Milk

**State bird:** Bluebird

**State fish:** Brook trout

**State flower:** Rose

**State fossil:** *Eurypterus remipes,* an extinct relative of the sea scorpion and king crab

**State fruit:** Apple

**State gem:** Garnet

**State insect:** Ladybug

**State muffin:** Apple muffin

**State shell:** Bay scallop

**State tree:** Sugar maple

State flag

State seal

## STATE SONG

### "I Love New York"

*Words and music by Steve Karmen*

I love New York,
I love New York,
I love New York.
There isn't another like it
No matter where you go
And nobody can compare it.
It's win and place and show.
New York is special.
New York is diff'rent
'Cause there's no place else on earth
Quite like New York
And that's why
I love New York,
I love New York,
I love New York.

38

# FAMOUS PEOPLE

Abdul-Jabbar, Kareem (1947– ), basketball player

Arnold, Tedd (1949– ), children's author and illustrator

Balanchine, George (1904–1983), dancer and choreographer

Ball, Lucille (1911–1989), actor

Carle, Eric (1929– ), children's author and illustrator

Combs, Sean "P. Diddy" (1971– ), rapper and clothing designer

Cruise, Tom (1962– ), actor

Gehrig, Lou (1903–1941), baseball player

Gershwin, George (1898–1937), pianist and composer

Giuliani, Rudy (1944– ), former mayor of New York

Gleason, Jackie (1916–1987), entertainer

Irving, Washington (1783–1859), author

Jordan, Michael (1963– ), basketball player

Lombardi, Vince (1913–1970), football coach

Rockwell, Norman (1894–1978), painter and illustrator

Roosevelt, Eleanor (1884–1962), first lady and humanitarian

Roosevelt, Franklin D. (1882–1945), U.S. president

Roosevelt, Theodore (1858–1919), U.S. president

Salk, Jonas (1914–1995), polio researcher

Stanton, Elizabeth Cady (1815–1902), suffragist

Truth, Sojourner (1797–1883), abolitionist and suffragist

Whitman, Walt (1819–1892), poet

# TO FIND OUT MORE

## At the Library

Burg, Ann E., and Maureen K. Brookfield (illustrator). *E Is for Empire: A New York State Alphabet*. Chelsea, Mich.: Sleeping Bear Press, 2003.

Curlee, Lynn. *Liberty*. New York: Atheneum Books for Young Readers, 2000.

Gerstein, Mordicai. *The Man Who Walked between the Towers*. Brookfield, Conn.: Roaring Brook Press, 2003.

Osborne, Mary Pope, Steve Johnson (illustrator), and Lou Fancher (illustrator). *New York's Bravest*. New York: A. A. Knopf, 2002.

Roth, Susan L. *It's a Dog's New York*. Washington, D.C.: National Geographic Society, 2001.

## On the Web

Visit our home page for lots of links about New York: *http://www.childsworld.com/links*

Note to Parents, Teachers, and Librarians: We routinely verify our Web links to make sure they are safe, active sites—so encourage your readers to check them out!

## Places to Visit or Contact

**Empire State Development Division of Tourism**
30 South Pearl Street
Albany, NY 12245
518/292-5100
*For more information about traveling in New York*

**New York State Museum**
Cultural Education Building
Albany, NY 12230
518/474-5877
*For more information about the history of New York*

# INDEX

Bye, Empire State.
We had a great time.
We'll come back soon!